# To My Children at Christmas

# To My Children at Christmas

Poems by

James Hannon

Cover design by Shay Culligan

ISBN: 978-1-63980-125-1

Kelsay Books
502 South 1040 East, A-119
American Fork, Utah 84003
Kelsaybooks.com

For Jessica

# Acknowledgments

The author gratefully acknowledges the editors of the following publications where these poems first appeared.

*Amethyst Journal:* "Drop in a Waterfall," "Two Ways of Looking at a Redbird"

*Ancient Paths:* "All Lies Should Bear the Weight of Lies"

*Anti-Heroin Chic:* "To My Children at Christmas"

*Blue River Review:* "Nauset Beach," "Surfacing"

*Braided Way:* "How Will You Help?"

*Cold Mountain Review:* "Ailanthus"

*Courtship of Winds:* "Sarajevo Monday"

*Ekstasis:* "Spring Planting"

*Gathered: Contemporary Quaker Poets:* "In Praise of Dangerous Women"

*Loch Raven Review:* "Invasive Species," "Nadia and the Uneven Bars"

*Pensive: A Global Journal of Spirituality and the Arts:* "Accident of Birth"

*Psaltery And Lyre:* "Go Along to Get Along"

*Rat's Ass Review:* "Kilifi All Day"

*Soundings East:* "Winter Birds"

*Vita Poetica:* "Satsang with Guruji"

*The Wayfarer:* "At the River"

*Words and Whispers:* "Johnny Appleseed"

*Zetetic:* "Annual Visit" "Forsake of Naming"

# Contents

# Johnny Appleseed

I was already five feeling pretty grown
when Johnny-next-door came into our yard.

My brother as often was mowing the lawn
as I watched and snacked on an apple.
When I finished, Johnny dared me twice
to throw the core at my bro.

Like Johnny my brother was twelve
and said don't!
I just started to laugh.
My brother was cool
so why should he care
if a little kid flipped him a core?

I threw and connected, and my life transformed.
My brother's blue irises turned to stone.
His words were few,
but he marched me through
the front door to see our dad.

I had never, ever feared my dad
but I learned something new that day.
He took the handoff and pulled me through
the doorway of my room,
me and my brother's room.
His words were none.
The spanks were hard and many.

Left alone on my bed
I bounced up and down
at five embarrassed by tears.

I cried, why, why,
what have I done?
Why have I been forsaken?
I double asked as I bounced up and down
but the only voice was my own.

# Hey, Dad

I was mad on those Saturday nights
when you weren't home and Mom
would drink too much and leave
the rolls too long in the oven
and start crying when Mike teased her.
She'd leave the kitchen and I'd follow her
to the living room where she'd throw
herself down on the couch to cry
some more and it was just so painful.

She had so little power and she knew it
and you knew it and Mike and I knew it.
But I knew it was wrong and you two didn't
and I had no power to get you to see it.

Or maybe you knew and lived with the guilt
because Helen needed you and you needed her
on Saturday nights after the long week.

It wasn't enough, that hour alone at the end
of the day, when she would go into your office
and close the door, the office with the big
leather recliner and the minibar that opened at four.

I understand why you wanted a second wife.
Mom was such a good Catholic she didn't know
how babies were made when you married
after seven years of dating.

Jesus, what did you talk about all that time?
What did Ireland and the Church do to you both?

When cancer took her breasts and threatened her life,
did anyone help you?

You had been in the war and were a man's man
and probably wouldn't have taken
the help that wasn't offered.

After all, you didn't cry when your mom died
when you were eight because Irish men don't cry.
They drink and offer it up for the souls in Purgatory.

There'd been thirty generations to practice
suffering with no power, and not enough food
after the times with no food
because the highly civilized landlords
took and took and gave back nothing.

Dad, you wouldn't want to hear
about generational trauma.
You'd say, you want sympathy?
It's in the dictionary
between stadium and symphony.

You were a pretty tough guy,
but you know what?
We had it, that generational trauma,
and the alcoholism and the coverups
and the fear of getting too close
and opening the heart
because we're sure life will break it.

I'm just glad you let me hug you near the end.

# In Praise of Dangerous Women

Long raven hair like Spanish moss
grabs a runaway slave in a Louisiana swamp—
bound fast to the mast
for his siren song,
like a horn through the fog
of a bayou bog where Morgan Le Fay
rises again from the mist
of his boyhood dreams.

Somehow, he pulls free
but his head is shorn—
like a nameless prison inmate
or a tonsured monk reborn
with a safer and holy name.
In the numinous light
of the piney woods,
*nel mezzo del cammin*
(as he understood)
he follows the trail,
like a well-bred hound,
of the sanguinous scent drifting
toward the ground.

When he gets to the crossroads
he tosses his bones
and to no one's surprise
those single point dice
stare up at him like the Siamese eyes
that called him out with a smoky smile.
She said some go that way and some go this.
He tastes her again when he bites his lip.

He had laughed years before at a bright-eyed man
who pulled his coat with a trembling hand
and rolled out a story of the horrible toll
of the triple Scorpio who stole his soul.
The broken man had sighed and let
his calling card reply—Blake's etching
of hell and an experienced verse:
the road of excess (may first make things worse
but it) leads to the palace of wisdom.

Stare at the sun.
Stare at a woman
who knows what she's done
and hasn't a single regret.
Reach behind yourself
for something to throw
through those black mirrored eyes.

Hear the blood rush in your ears.
Feel your feet tingle.
Feel your arms shake.
Scream 'til the rafters
threaten to break.

Breathe.

Breathe again.

Open your hands.
Laugh at yourself.
Begin.

# Satsang with Guruji

Can't you see that flight
is disloyalty to one's higher self,
that fight is a lack of humility,
and fear the sad absence of faith?

You've always known
you'd have to walk on the water
to get to where you long to be.

What good was your thinking
before I called you out?
You were frightened and lonely
and already far from home.

Back to your family?
Was your family always good to you?
Were they good *for* you?

In that painful space between doubt and faith
relief comes only in letting go
of the shame and fear that hold you back.
With love there is no shame or fear.

Do the angelfish in your aquarium
question the source of their food?
What can they know of the world
so rich and full outside their tank?
Could they ever understand
why and how you provide for them?

You complain that I honor your wife.
I give this lesson freely and with love.

You are unsettled by my watches and cars.
This is your idolatry—you worship an image
planted in your mind when you were a child.

What I offer is freedom.

Why don't you want to be free?

# Caged

Little sparrow,
precious pet of my darling,
she cuddles you in her lovely lap
and tempts you with her fingertip,
daring you to nip harder.

When our forbidden desires flare
too brightly I offer lighthearted talk
to relieve her frustration,
to help dim our painful
and burdensome passions.

But how can I be a comfort to her
when I am the source of her pain?

Better for me if I could be as pleased
as she to play with you, sparrow,
and not envy your favored position.

(After Catullus #2)

# Full Catastrophe Living

When the weight comes down to bend you
like a bough under snow in a winter storm,
don't be too proud for weeping
or to pray for a way to stay warm.

If the icy crust breaks beneath your feet
and the river agrees to sweep you away,
the call has come, and your journey's begun
into terror incognita.

Try to avoid these questions:
Why now? Why me? Why not someone else?
Don't rely on your strength as a swimmer,
great effort and will won't help.

Time to go with the flow and incline to supine.
Inhale in that space between water and ice,
exhale very slow to get panic control.
Even still, you may not survive.

A hidden sandbar could save you.
Tattered and scattered, scramble to shore.
That's where you could find some helpers—
the uncanny, peculiar, unholy, divine.

Open your ears to women,
the gray ones grown way beyond care.
They will say a few words in passing
you may have only one chance to hear.

Find a place where you can get some sleep.
Eat wherever food is shared.
Work and hang out with the homeless,
you will meet a few river vets there.

This could be the real thing or merely a test,
maybe a lesson or dance.
If you start to feel rage, please remember
when you did ask for just one more chance.

# My Neighbor Schools Me on Invasive Species

I haven't lived here long
but I can read the history of my back woods.
A stand of beech and birch, primary growth,
have been strangled by Multiflora Rosa
and Oriental Bittersweet.

Don't be impressed by their beauty.
These invaders crowd out the natives,
entwine and drag our trees to their knees.
Look here—a tangle of bizarre couplings.

It's not enough to strip the vines
and uproot the bushes.
They'll only grow back, and quickly.
That's where the Roundup comes in.
Even so, we must remain vigilant.

The work is hard, but it pleases me
to be out here with my daughters
to teach them the difference between
old growth and new,
how to beat back the invasives
before they deform our woods
into a hopeless snake pit.

It will not be the work of one summer
but in time our land will be restored,
and I will leave my children an estate
to make any great family proud.

# Go Along to Get Along *

Don't think about the Holocaust.

No, really. Don't.

Don't think about
genocide
slavery
Hiroshima
napalm.

Because if you do,
you'll probably think too much
(you know you!).
And then when some nice lady says
God is good
or
Everything happens for a reason

you might say something.

Even if she nods and allows
that, yes, there are some mysteries,
she'll dismiss you as rude and self-important.

And here's the thing.
You will not be the angel of her epiphany.
You are not a guardian of the galaxy
and you're certainly not a Time Lord.

What's done is done.

If you say this something at a party
you might not be invited to another.

You could become isolated and embittered
and miss out on the treats.
Now, if some nice fellow recounting
his life-changing experience tells you

It was a terrible accident
but God must have had
something special planned for me
because I survived
though my friend did not.

Do not think about your lovely friend
whose rear axle broke in two
on the Florida Turnpike,
flipping her car on its head
and her head, breaking both.

Do not think about your friend
whose son died at five
after three years of cancer treatments.

God must not have had something special
planned for them.

And what would you say?
Quote Shakespeare…
they kill us for their sport?
Probe the theodicy dilemma?

Tell him about your friends?
Ask him whether God listens
to the prayers of a Jew?

No, it's better to say nothing.

* *If you want to get along, you have to go along* is the advice that House Speaker Sam Rayburn (and later Tip O'Neill) gave to newcomers in the House of Representatives.

# Accident of Birth

It was the smell of his skin
and the unfiltered Camels
in the pocket of his starched white shirt
as I burrowed into
the safest place on earth.

It was the introduction to the Garden
and Fenway and getting to Yankee Stadium
for the '58 Series
and his reassurance,
when my brother teased me,
that the Yankees would not come back
from 3 games to 1
and it didn't matter later
when they did.

It was the stories he told me at night
on my bed about the war,
his ship and his fear
and how he seemed
to tell them only to me.
And how he would check my closet
without making me feel bad for asking.

It was getting up at six for daily mass in Lent—
the awful feeling of the cold and dark
but a time alone with him,
away from my mother's voice.

And later
even with the arguments about the unjust war
that could have killed me

even with his votes for Nixon and Ford
and the pinky ring he started to wear in his fifties

even with his absent Saturday nights
when I had to comfort my weeping mother

even with his complaints about welfare cheats
while he worked under the table
for the men he was paid to investigate

even though he wouldn't sell the house
to a black family
because it wouldn't be fair to the neighbors

I couldn't help myself.

# Feet of Clay

When the sins of others come to mind
my response, I find, is seldom kind.
I rejoice to see those feet of clay —
they justify my wayward way.

For if sanctity is always fraud
what need have I of grace and God?
My freedom ticket's been re-punched.
My critics? A hypocritical bunch.

# Yes, Yes, That Would Be Treason

Yes, yes, yes, yes, our fathers betrayed us cuz
they were so eager to prove how manly and
American they were with their booze, cigs, flags,
and secretary mistresses and no time for us cuz
they worked *so hard* **but** stopped off for a quick
one on the way home or went to see a man about
a horse while our mothers banged pots or cried
and our fathers rolled eyes at them for being *so
goddamn emotional* and the very worst thing to be
was *girly* so we had to *man up,* but we could never
be tough enough even with the fights we won or
lost cuz there would always be some we backed
away from so we had to be in charge with girls and be
sure to *get some* (even if they *said* they didn't want to)
cuz a man goes and gets what he wants unless he
reads too much **but** you gotta dress well for church
cuz that looks good **but** don't take church too seriously
cuz that's for women and then came

*Vietnam*

and they needed us to go to prove how patriotic they
were and what good fathers they were cuz a good
father doesn't raise a coward or someone who doesn't
love this country, the best country, or raise a communist
cuz that's as bad as a sissy, and they *would* be proud
of us and love us if we were willing to die in a jungle
but they still wouldn't have much time for us cuz work
and golf and mistresses and everything and men don't
do that or hug because *sissy* and *no son of mine.*

And they told us to stay away from those protests cuz
the government will get your name and stay away
from Negroes cuz drugs and crime *and your sisters* and
they destroy property values so we *couldn't* sell the house
to one of them cuz that wouldn't be fair to our neighbors
in the Knights of Columbus, like Mr. McKenna, who was
so proud cuz *his son,* Kevin, went to West Point and
Vietnam and got his jaw shot off and the McKennas
became the envy of the parish. And it *was* too bad
about his face **but** a good girl married him, and she was
definitely a virgin and strongly pro-life. And Kevin said
that the guys who went to Canada could *never* come back
cuz they committed *treason.*

# Vermont Solstice

Light brighter than the sun
pierced the midsummer night.
Thunder boomed over the mountains.
We counted the storm's distance
in seconds and clicks.
How far away the strike.
How much time to get to safety.

Fireflies danced unconcerned above
the lawn, a more constant, inconsistent
illumination of the night.

We rented that Airbnb cottage
from a Vietnam vet who wakes each day
in those mountains and thinks
of all the terrible things happening
all over the world and wonders
how he got to be so lucky.

I got lucky once and drew #276.
I forget passwords and phone numbers
more often now but not that one.
It's shorter but I don't think that's why.

I know men my age with a backpack
of memories of pant-shitting terror,
of counting backwards slowly from 365,
still wondering why the hell they were there,
blaming themselves for being punked,
and still expected to salute the flag and forget
about the killing and the bombing
and the dead buddies.

Real men don't talk about war, some say,
to protect their families, to be paternal.

They don't talk about it because they
can't afford to dig too deeply
into the betrayal, into Abraham and Isaac,
into presidents and Congressmen
who didn't give a shit about them
or the jobs they helped move
to the Philippines, Mexico, El Salvador,
Vietnam.

A firefly got stuck in the ceiling of the cottage porch.
It flashed as it crawled along the edge of a board
but couldn't find its way out.
My wife and I wanted to free it but then thought,
one firefly, why bother, but we felt compelled.
I found a broom and swept it out of a crack
between two boards and it danced and flashed
in front of us and made its way back into the night.

# Red Giant

It sure was hot yesterday—
94 degrees in September.
Seems like the global warming folks are right.

Today it's 54.
Hey, it's New England.
Don't like the weather?
Wait a minute!!

The astrophysicists say one thing's for certain.
Eventually the sun will expand
and turn our planet into a desert,
the uninhabitable kind.

That's before the sun absorbs the earth completely.

God did give Noah the rainbow sign—
no more water, the fire next time.

Some of us knew it all along—
the arc is long, and it bends towards annihilation.

…more study may be required.

# Sarajevo Monday

Waken at dawn
to a muezzin's call
from a nearby minaret.
*Hayya alas Salah*
*Hayya alal Falah*
Hurry to the prayer.
Rise up for salvation.
Prayer is better than sleep.

Follow footprints in the sand
of Sarajevo sidewalks
where mortar can still fall
from the walls above you,
to the market where mortars
lobbed from hillsides mingled
animal, vegetable, mineral.
Among your twenty questions—
is it a species that kills for pleasure?

See the roses painted
on sidewalks where victims fell.
That cemetery sprouts rows
of identical white stiles.

Now to the old town
where young Muslim women
have colored their hair
fuchsia, magenta, crimson.
Walk past ruins of a caravanserai
to the ancient bazaar cornered by
a cathedral, a mosque, a synagogue.

A collective effort feeds
the wild dogs at the market
They seem wary of strangers
but they know their friends.

Walk down Ferhadija Street
to where you're welcomed into
the courtyard of the old mosque.
Please observe the symbols:
no smoking, no short skirts, no guns.

In a cafe hear the death metal rap of Necro
"I'll hit that pussy up with a nasty attack"
followed by Marley's "One Love."

Up in the hills after-school children
play around a broken fountain.
Behind them eighty names
are carved in a marble wall—
wide-ranging birth years
and a three-year range for deaths.
Izmeta, Razija, Mehmed.

A chubby boy is teased by the others.
Two adults, maybe teachers,
encourage him to re-engage,
and stay to watch.
The children play again.

# Kilifi Saturday

Noonday ravens swoop up to rooftops
where scarlet bright bougainvillea droop
down to the market stalls below.

Kenyan women love their bodies
as they swing and sway across the street,
laughing and calling to each other.

From the swaps and shops
gospel and reggae sing faith and joy.

Why is everyone smiling?

Swindlers white and black
swore to promote and protect,
then picked their pockets
but could reach no further.

# Fragmented

we speak quickly now
in fragments in tweets
in disappearing stories
no time for more than

broken words as
thoughts break into thoughts
in the painful witnessing way
look at me thinking
this thought is worth
thinking when there are so many
thinkers with their own thoughts to think
even in my head.

irony for a dishonest cynical time
or is this just a style that finds its time
from time to time in the cycle of styles
so a new generation can marvel and preen?

but where could we go beyond this point,
this blind alley labyrinth, this ouroboros?
straightforward sentiment is risible
this close to the Holocaust and then
the other holocausts.

if faith in progress died at the Somme,
what died in Vietnam and Rwanda,
Bosnia and Iraq before coherence
offed herself on cable news?

we may be called to hope,
never to surrender but in our castles
we huddle in fear of the Huns and Goths
who arrive at the end of an empire
to euthanize it.

do we have a pope or a queen
to go out and parley for peace?
who can negotiate with a plague or a flood?
or should we gather to flagellate,
to atone for our greatest sin?
is that our greed, our sloth,
or our despair?

# All Lies Should Bear the Weight of Lies

All lies should bear the weight of lies,
nothing foreseen by a cynical spouse
or dubious public immune to surprise.
Each lie should shatter the night,
unimagined 'til understood,
with shock for every deception
in hearts more accustomed to truth.

A kiss should bear the weight of a kiss,
no cosmetic to cover our scorn
or deception to muffle a serpentine hiss.
A kiss can win back the night
from the paralyzing terror
of the loss of ourselves in each other's eyes —
that ancient, repetitive error.

All fights should bear the weight of fights,
no half measures once well begun
when the stakes are as high as human rights.
A good fight can beat back the night—
holy anger still makes tyrants tremble.
And nothing's more powerful than the sound
of a righteous people assembled.

All deaths should bear the weight of death,
a thunderous loss to those who knew
the singular virtues, the height and breadth.
Each death should waken the night,
well-imagined, never denied,
still with the power to take our breath
like a spear thrust into a side.

# I Speak for the Current

I speak for the current
running beneath your feet
burning and churning,
the molten irresistible

with your ear to the ground
can you hear the sound
of a distant locomotive?
can you feel the rumble
of the plates?

can you feel anything?

pleased that you can't see us
we celebrate our underneathness
our joyous bubbling life down under

we don't need to be seen to reshape the world.
our name is alchemical—*solve et coagula.*

your mantle of glaciers is a puddle to us
our ceaseless heat melts resistance
builds mountains where we emerge
to shock and awe as we laugh to hear
no one could have seen this coming

we have always been coming
always beneath your feet

flowing

expanding

exploding

# Nauset Beach

The wind is still today.
Seagulls and sandpipers tiptoe
through us and around us
en pounce for a careless mistake.
An old man wheels in his chair
to watch a pair of gulls and smiles
to see them so close and so free.

Everyone on the beach except
my granddaughters is white.
Should this wreck my day like
shivered timbers on the shore?
The girls don't seem to notice or care.

We breast the waves but swim
in water no deeper than our waists
because we swim with the sharks.
Their flag is unfurled
and seals swim a few yards beyond us,
the size and color of my girls.

The Cape waves are warming
and the tide is still coming in.
The sharks are here to stay.
We're learning to live with them.

# Too Fond of Myself

When I grow too fond of my knowledge,
my wisdom and savoir faire,
I consider a clot in my bloodstream
and how quickly they'd all disappear.

I'd still be the same person then, I think,
with all those fine qualities gone,
and worthy of love and respect, I hope,
without all the carrying on.

# Uneven Bars

Back arched, feet nearly en pointe,
her arms relaxed at her sides,
she narrows her vision to bars
that could have been made for pain.

She sees the immediate future,
her mastery of her fear,
bows her head slightly and springs
to the first bar and up, with a grace

we could have expected
but with power unforeseen.
Atop the high bar her feet reach
for the sky where she pauses

and we hear the crowd gasp
into the pause between inhale and out,
the no time eternally now.

We're allowed to share this perfection,
the grace of a saint and reminder
of something too precious to name.

Fourteen and a perfect ten—
she drops to the ground as intended
with a twisting turning dismount.

Where could she backflip from here?
She could only go down
to the greed and grasp of the handlers,

the owners, bosses, and despots
who profit from exploitation
and children turned inside out

Locked inside her own country,
forbidden to leave except
to perform for national glory
and to strengthen a madman's reign.

But flexible strength is hard to break.
Over mountains in moonlight
she made her escape to a new land,
new troubles and a fight again to be free.

She stumbled but regained her balance
as she'd always been able to do
and showed us a dispensation
from all our demands to be tens.

So, we learn it's no shame to be human
and to need some help from a friend.
And yes, it's not that we fall from perfection
but how well we rise up again.

# In Praise of Lyn Lifshin (1942–2019)

I thought her poems would keep her afloat
forever, or at least until I could meet her
while she was wearing a pair of her sexy boots,
maybe at a writers' retreat
where there's really a chance
to connect.

I wouldn't have cared that she was older
than her photos (who isn't?) because she was so
prolific.

Of course, she mailed it in some of the time
with the quick pieces while riding on a train
about what was going by and naming the towns.
I still wanted to read her
because she could be so good
and had created a persona
greater than the sum of its parts
even though there were so many parts.

Could a man do that?
Cultivate a sexy persona,
be that sexy in print and photo performance?

How can we be free
if we resent a woman
for having more sex than we do,
for being sexy and loving it?

What is more poetic than eros,
than the drive
to touch to have
to be had
to win to lose

and come back again to win,
to play, to massage the air
between two people
who can dance the dance
and feel the rush?

What's more poetic than great sex?

I would have complimented her boots
and she would have laughed or not
(polite or bored, now I'll never know)
and maybe she'd have written a quick poem
about the old guy with a lame game
but I would have been up close smitten
and that would have been enough.

Kudos, Lyn, for the poems and the fashion.
Thanks for letting us know
we don't always have to worry a tenth draft,
that we can let our hair down
change the color
wear some cool hats
and buy a new pair of boots,
if you know what I mean.

I'm sorry I missed you
and I already miss you.

# The Bishop of Armagh

There were no snakes on the island
when the kidnapped lad came aground
except for those who walked erect
and contended for the crown.

Boy to man, six years a slave
often naked, cold, alone,
he tended sheep against the threats—
the savage known, the worse unknown.

Isolation draws a mind in deep
to face temptation and despair,
to rage against one's enemies,
and find a way back into prayer.

In the hermit's hut a soul was formed,
hammered and peened as from a searing forge.
Quenched in tears a new man was born—
faith over fear, love over scorn.

As sheep have neither wit nor strength
to save them from the wolf,
they gambol off full unaware
of how some lies appear as truth.

A good shepherd knows his sheep
from the fleece down to the bone.
They may belong to someone else
but he loves them as his own.

So, once freed he returned to the verdant land,
first his exile, now his home,
and took up the crozier and his cross
to save their souls for Rome.

Patrick preached the way of peace
and the soul that's born again,
founded churches, schools, and abbeys
and new life for women and men.

Irish monks would save the West
when the lamp of learning was elsewhere lost.
The nation would raise many scholars and saints,
and defenders of justice no matter the cost.

A man in his time does just what he can,
the future is always unknown.
But Ireland's still grateful for that long ago
when he claimed them as his own.

# Ailanthus

Gritty and graceful,
you bloom where
you're not planted
and prove that a tree
can grow anywhere.
Unabashed by your
surroundings, never
scandalized by your
companions and so
well-adjusted to the
smog and sooty view.

I find your virtue tiresome.

But like fireworks
each of your explosions
renews the wonder.
How could a tree grow there?
On dust, on asphalt,
through a fence?
Do other trees demand
too much?

I could unearth you
and toss you into
a rusting dumpster
but you'd only take root
and mock my ill humor.

I would ignore you
but you take me by surprise
with my resistance lowered

as I round a darkening corner
and catch you waving
in the corner of my eye.

# Forsake of Naming

Pretend that I charge you
to name all the creatures,
great and small, leaf and limb,
so you can feel in control
of your outer world when
so much inside is unnamable.

Your numberless descendants
will count and classify kingdoms
they think they rule.
Dominion they will call it
like one of their orders of angels.

It will be orders and ranks
columns and rows
greater than and less than
until some learn
that which is named
is no longer itself.

Then will begin the unknowing.

# Drop in a Waterfall

Who tells me
being a drop
in a waterfall
is not enough?

Must I shine like a sun
so my planets can orbit
around me?

Or be an angel
at the top of the tree?

What is so terrible
about being part of the flow,
one among many?

What is the ocean,
my fellow droplets,
but all of us finally together?

# Lot's Nameless Wife

Oh, go ahead and look.

Who wouldn't want to dig
her life story—to get what's true
and what was a song and dance?

Maybe Lot just got busted
with another man's wife
and had to lickety-split.
You know a cat
can always kick up some dust
to cover his shit.
Remember how Lot played it before,
me or your lyin' eyes, you silly girl?

And sister Eve,
please, eat the freakin' apple.
What kind of person runs
from the knowledge of good and evil?
A case of arrested development,
that's what.

Let's get clear on this guilt and fear business.
We're supposed to blindly obey what?
Kiss the slippers of a puppet-master
who made us and then condemns us
for being what we are?
Ha-ha. Ridic!

Here's what I got for that.
Someone wants to turn me
into a pillar of salt?
Go ahead.
Then lick me.

# Marriage Therapy

When you're ash and the dust has settled
and the kids have selected their rugs,
no more need to test your mettle
in the battle you called love.

You can rest assured eternally
that you never, ever gave in.
You preserved your pride and dignity—
to surrender would have been sin.

# At the River

In that desert space they finally met
upon the banks, still soaking wet.
Then days of grace they'd not forget
in the days of torture coming yet.

Such talks they had by that riverbed,
those two who knew that to be led
to lead, to bleed, to lose one's head
is the only way to raise the dead.

It takes hope to value humankind
when many lag so far behind,
to kin and strangers so unkind,
but they could not leave them helpless, blind.

For those who have turned their backs to lies
there is no need for long goodbyes.
No tears to shed, no desperate sighs.
The way is clear in each other's eyes.

# Spring Planting

Ground must be plowed
for the seed to be sown
but the turf cries out
with a dreadful moan
against this inversion
of all it has known.

Why here, why us
the grasses cry.
What have we done
that we must die?

Oh, my friends, you'll see,
I can swear by God,
it's your soil that counts
even more than your sod.
New life more splendid
than familiar grass,
sweet fruit and bright flowers
will bloom at last.

Not without effort
and not without pain,
but the harvest will bring
inconceivable gain.

# Annual Visit

My sister's farm looks different
again this year.
The old elm finally dropped
and the bobolinks didn't
return to the high meadow.
The peaches are poor, but she says
next year should be better.

The sky is the same in its usual way
of shifting clouds and colors.
I went wading in the brook
this morning and it felt a little smaller
with the loosestrife closing in like
plaque on the farm's lone artery.

I walked behind the barn to find
the medicine wheel we built last year.
Lines of pebbles to the four directions
will stay true for millennia if
they remain that long undisturbed.

I threw one of the stones high
and deep into the west woods.
It would have taken months
for a glacier to move it that far.

Out here in the orchard
I look and listen
for Eve, for Lilith.
Feed me your fruit.
Give me your lips so I can fully
taste this day, this rapture.
Then push me through
a tear in the veil.

I know how we were shielded
in our Edens.
I've seen the leaves fall,
the elm tree toppled.
I ask only to live today,
as full of juice as your peaches,
to shout and sing
thank you! thank you!
fearless and joyful.

Then I could learn
to return to the earth,
satisfied and grateful.

# How Will You Help?

I woke in the middle of the night
to a vision I didn't know I had desired.

A young, dark-skinned woman
in a light blue hijab and long white robe
took my left hand and slowly drew me
through my bedroom window.
She wanted to show me something.
I knew I would follow her anywhere.

We floated slowly it seemed but
the ground passed quickly beneath us.
Looking down through the night sky
I had many questions, but I soon understood
her silent language of movement and gesture.
*Trust me completely. Be patient.*

Her free hand would sometimes extend
toward the ground and we would descend
to see illuminated families, children at play,
other children crying.

We stopped to hover over a broad forest.
Slowly my vision focused.
I saw men and women
running through the night,
carrying their crying and screaming children.
As they ran fire fell from the sky
and the forest ignited behind them.
I could not tell if they would outrun the flames.

My chest tightened as did my grip on her hand.
She floated closer to me and kissed my forehead.
I felt my chest break open like a shell.
I was overcome with love and pain.

She released my hand and pointed to the ground
*What*, I wondered?
She held my gaze with loving eyes.
I felt her response. *How will you help?*

# To My Children at Christmas

For Christmas this year
I am giving you my heart.
Besides you and your mother
it is my only treasure.

Inside is all I have felt
and learned from standing
outside and knocking on doors
that would not
or could not open.

That was pain
but it's all right now.
I understand
and I hope you will too.
It helps to remember
that sometimes
we are the ones inside
unable to open the door.

You'll probably think this is corny
but I can live with that.
I thought about socks
again this year
but I figure you have enough.

# Winter Birds

It was the year I quit coffee,
five years after booze
and four years after cigarettes.

I shoveled the whole driveway
in a January blizzard
and my middle-aged, momentarily
caffeine free heart
made not a murmur of protest.
I felt like a righteous Mormon,
Brigham Young on the edge of the desert.
I wanted to go back in the house
and make another baby with you
but it was past time for that.

Susanna bundled out to help
plowing through snow almost to her waist.
We heard crows complaining overhead
as they always do in snow.
A blue jay hopped by, ignoring us,
and chickadees screamed at the feeder
across the street.

It suddenly struck her,
"Haven't they gone south yet?"
I told her that some stay all year.
She finished a path
with her bright red shovel
and went back inside.

In a minute I felt tired
and wanted a smoke.
I watched the snowfall slow
and collect on my glasses.

I caught for a moment that smell
of wet childhood winters,
stamped my boots
and started on the cars.

# Two Ways of Looking at a Redbird

*Such is the constitution of all things, or such the plastic
power of the human eye, that the primary forms, as the
sky, the mountain, the tree, the animal, give us a delight
in and of themselves…*

*Nature always wears the colors of the spirit.*
—Ralph Waldo Emerson, from *Nature*


The dab of vivid red is a grace note
in the snowy landscape, a painting,
a photograph waiting to be made.
It is *cardinalis cardinalis,* its bold color
a surprising result of evolution,
one mutation after another,
some that work out better than others
and voila! the bright northern cardinal.
There is a delightful fit between
the cardinal and my lens, retina, brain.
The natural world pleases us so much
because we evolved together.
Our visual capabilities and aesthetic sense
have been shaped by ten thousand
generations of mutation and natural selection.
Homo sapiens and cardinalis belong together.

The dab of vivid red is a grace note
in the snowy landscape, a painting,
a photograph waiting to be made.
The cardinal may be hidden from the hawk
but we can hear his trills
as he hops from branch to branch
in our overgrown thicket
on the shortest, darkest day
when the weary year lies down to die,

like a wise elephant who knows
she has had enough of this life.
Then in a flash he flares upward
through the overcast sky with the color
of the rising sun
and the rainbow promise we still need to hear—
the dark will not last forever.

# Surfacing

The towering beech is a shimmering ocean
of purple and green where its limbs
stretch high above the white-haired man
supine beneath its treetop crown.

The ground beneath him hums
as he measures the depths of the ocean
receding in that windblown tide.
Sound muffles as his body lifts slowly
to part the waves washing his face like
the cilia soothing the tide within him.

Rocking through the ocean toward the light,
vertebrae loosened by the sea, he's a merman,
gliding and flipping on his pivot center,
no longer up or down, east or west.
Breathing more with gills than lungs
he bobs atop the sea and rises slowly
in an azure sky, diffusing like a cloud.

Time and space dive over
each other like dolphins.

In the slow silence of space,
he feels the faint beating of blood
and the tug of the spacewalker
who recalls an old promise.
He hears again the murmur
of the faraway earth
to which he turns again in time,
tumbling, remembering, surfacing.

# About the Author

James Hannon is a psychotherapist in Massachusetts where he accompanies adolescents and adults who are recovering from addictions and mood disorders and seeking meaningful and joyful lives. His poems have appeared in *Blue Lake Review, Blue River, Cold Mountain Review, Soundings East,* and other journals and in *Gathered: Contemporary Quaker Poets.* His collection, *The Year I Learned the Backstroke,* was published by Aldrich Press.

www.ingramcontent.com/pod-product-compliance
Lightning Source LLC
Chambersburg PA
CBHW071357090426
42738CB00012B/3147